# THE
# Mississippian
# Culture

## THE MOUND
## BUILDERS

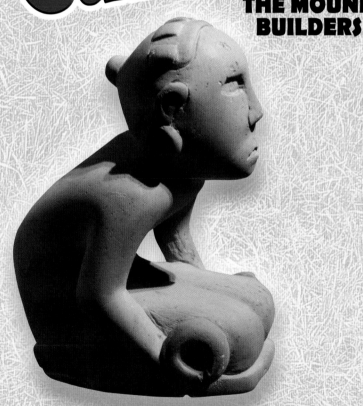

Louise Spilsbury

Gareth Stevens
PUBLISHING

Please visit our website, www.garethstevens.com.

For a free color catalog of all our high-quality books, call toll free 1-800-542-2595 or fax 1-877-542-2596.

Cataloging-in-Publication Data

Names: Spilsbury, Louise.
Title: The Mississippian culture: the mound builders / Louise Spilsbury.
Description: New York : Gareth Stevens Publishing, 2019. | Series: Analyze the ancients | Includes glossary and index.
Identifiers: LCCN ISBN 9781538225677 (pbk.) | ISBN 9781538225660 (library bound)
Subjects: LCSH: Mississippian culture--Juvenile literature. | Indians of North America--Antiquities--Juvenile literature.
Classification: LCC E99.M6815 S646 2019 | DDC 977.3--dc23

First Edition

Published in 2019 by
Gareth Stevens Publishing
111 East 14th Street, Suite 349
New York, NY 10003

© 2019 Gareth Stevens Publishing

1/19 Apple $23.95 JNF

Produced for Gareth Stevens by Calcium Creative Ltd
Editors: Sarah Eason and Jennifer Sanderson
Designers: Paul Myerscough and Jessica Moon
Picture researcher: Rachel Blount

Picture credits: Cover: Wikimedia Commons: Daderot; Inside: Flickr: Carolyn Cuskey: pp. 10, 37; Jimmy Smith: p. 34; Goodfreephotos.com: pp. 16, 20, 21; Shutterstock: Jeffrey M. Frank: p. 5; Igorsm8: p. 14; Ronald Wilfred Jansen: p. 26; JB Manning: p. 4; Melnikof: p. 7; Joseph Sohm: pp. 6, 19; Vladimir Shutter: p. 28; Warat42: p. 38; Wikimedia Commons: Altairisfar (Jeffrey Reed): pp. 13, 33; Scott Bauer, USDA: p. 39; Marc Carlson: p. 31; Peter Coxhead: p. 29; Daderot: pp. 25, 32; FA2010: pp. 1, 22-23; Jflo23: pp. 11, 12; Ken Lund: p. 17; NYPL: p. 43; Kevin Payravi: p. 24; William H. Powell/US Capitol: p. 42; QuartierLatin1968: p. 27; Herb Roe, www.chromesun.com: pp. 15, 36; Heironymous Rowe: p. 8; James Steakley: p. 18; TimVickers: pp. 9, 41; Uyvsdi: pp. 30, 45; Walters Art Museum/Gift of the Austen-Stokes Ancient Americas Foundation, 2007: p. 35.

Printed in the United States of America

CPSIA compliance information: Batch #CS18GS: For further information, contact Gareth Stevens, New York, New York at 1-800-542-2595.

# CONTENTS

# CHAPTER 1

# People of the River

In about AD 800, an important **culture** developed along the Mississippi River. They lived in what is now the southeastern United States. The group of Native Americans who settled there is named for the mighty Mississippi River. Their culture grew, and so did the earth mounds they built. The Mississippi Mound Builders developed an important and powerful **civilization** that lasted until about AD 1500.

## River of Life

This ancient civilization built its mounds and towns on a large area along the Mississippi River. The Mississippi is one of the world's major river systems. It is also the longest river in North America. It flows 2,340 miles (3,766 km) south from Minnesota and joins the sea just below present-day New Orleans. Every time the river flooded its banks, it brought water to the strips of land beside it. The river also washed **fertile** mud onto this area of soil. The Mississippians were mainly farmers, and this rich soil allowed them to grow enough crops to feed their growing populations.

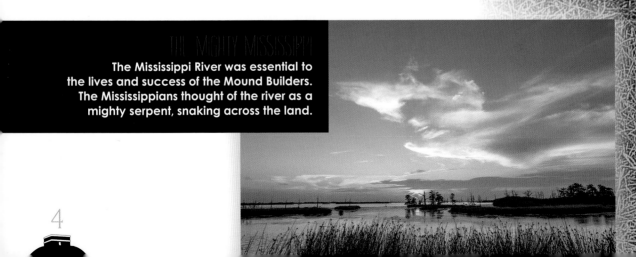

**THE MIGHTY MISSISSIPPI**
The Mississippi River was essential to the lives and success of the Mound Builders. The Mississippians thought of the river as a mighty serpent, snaking across the land.

# Mississippian Cultures

There were several different Native American groups living in this region at this time. They include the Chickasaw, Choctaw, and Natchez. These peoples shared a lot in common. They all made large mounds, with different buildings on top. They all grew large amounts of corn. This allowed them to feed large populations of people. It also allowed some people to do jobs other than farming. These jobs included making arts and crafts, or governing the region. Many of the Mississippians had a similar style of pottery. It used shells found in the river or sea. They all took part in trade with each other and across much of America. They also performed similar religious ceremonies. Each town and the villages around it were ruled by a powerful chief and his relatives.

# Rise of the Mound Builders

The early Mississippi cultures developed from the Native American Woodland way of life. That way of life existed from about AD 500 to AD 1000. These peoples are now known as Woodland tribes. They lived, made shelters, and found food in the forests near lakes or streams. Gradually, different groups began to settle in one area for longer. They also began to grow crops. These early Mississippians lived from around AD 1000 to AD 1200.

## The Mississippian Culture

The Mississippian culture often refers to the Middle Mississippi period. That time period was the peak of the Mississippian culture. At the time, some centers, such as Cahokia in present-day Illinois, expanded. They became vast cities where important ceremonies were held. Mounds were fairly common. But at that time, almost every town had at least one large mound. There was also a more complex way of life. A town and the villages around were it ruled by a chief and a few of the **elite** people. They ruled thousands of people across an area called a **chiefdom**. Gradually, a Mississippian religion, art, and **symbols** spread between different chiefdoms. This period lasted from around AD 1200 to AD 1400.

**WOODLAND MOUNDS**

**Burial mounds were especially common among Native Americans from the Woodland period.**

The Mississippian culture thrived because the people started farming corn, beans, and squash. That allowed populations to grow. The people settled in or around major centers or towns.

# The Late Mississippi Period

From AD 1400, the Mississippian culture started to falter. There were more wars between chiefdoms. Evidence has shown that more towns built fences or trenches to protect the people from attacks. There was less mound building, too, which suggests there was less time for ceremonies. Those ceremonies held communities together and made them feel part of a united **society**. People also started moving away from some of the most important centers, such as Cahokia. That may have been because of the wars. Or, changes in weather may have made it harder for farmers to grow food to feed all the people.

# Examining Evidence

The Mississippian Mound Builders had no system for writing records of their lives. They did not leave behind stone monuments or buildings as some ancient cultures did. However, we can still learn about how they lived and who they were. We can study the mounds they built and examine other evidence.

## Archaeologists at Work

Archaeologists are scientists who study the evidence of past human lives. The Mississippians left behind some large mounds. The mounds are easy to find at sites such as Cahokia in Illinois, Moundville in Alabama, Angel Site in Indiana, Kincaid in Illinois, Aztalan in Wisconsin, and Spiro in Oklahoma. We can also still see the large holes, called borrow pits. These were left in areas where soil was dug out to make the mounds. Archaeologists dig up and discover items inside the mounds, or in the ground nearby. These tell them how the people lived. They also study written accounts from European explorers. Those men arrived in the region at the end of the Mississippian era.

### MISSISSIPPIAN PEOPLE

These stone figures were found at the Etowah Indian Mounds site in Georgia. It is believed they could represent important figures in the culture's history.

# Uncovering a Culture

The Mississippians were excellent potters. They left behind thousands of pots and other interesting **artifacts**. Pottery in the shape of people shows us what they looked like. It also shows us what they wore and what things were important to them. Archaeologists can tell what pots were used for, depending on where they were found. Some were found in **temples**, so they tell us about religious ceremonies. They are also carefully carved. So that tells us the things the figures are shown holding or doing must have been very important to the people and their way of life.

## ANALYZE THE ANCIENTS

This figure of a kneeling woman with a basket and a corn plant at her side was found in a temple. Based on the information you have learned, can you answer these questions? Check your conclusions against the Answers on pages 44–45.

1. This figure was found in a temple. What does this tell us about what the figure was used for?

2. This carefully carved figure is shown with corn. What does the corn tell us?

# CHAPTER 2

# Chiefdoms and Commoners

One of the important parts of the Mississippian Mound Builder culture was their society. It was organized into **ranks**. The highest rank was the chief and the lowest was the commoners.

## Rulers and Followers

Mississippian societies were structured as chiefdoms. The chief held almost all the power. Most chiefs were men, but there were female leaders, too. Below the chiefs were the nobles or elites, who were usually related to the chief. Chiefdoms were hereditary. That means they were passed from one generation to the next. Usually when a chief died or became too old to lead, his eldest son took his place. Most of the people were commoners—the lowest rank of people. They had little or no power. They were usually farmers, craftspeople, and laborers.

### COMMON CRAFTSPEOPLE

Commoners were often craftspeople. They used materials such as marine shells to make ornaments. This necklace and these beads are made from shells.

## Corn and the Chief

The chief's power may have come from the way he was able to control the corn crop. Corn was an important crop and a **staple** of the Mississippian diet. This meant that if a crop failed because of a drought, for example, the people could starve. However, corn was fairly easy to store and could be dried and kept for a long time. So the chief collected part of every harvest and kept it in storage. He could bring it out to feed the people during the winter when food was scarce, or if a harvest failed.

**AN IMPORTANT CHIEF**

**This is a modern statue depicting a chief of the Etowah Indian Mounds site in Georgia. Chiefs held the power in the Mississippian Mound-Builder culture.**

## Powerful Elites

Some Mississippian peoples believed that their chief was related to the sun. They called him the Great Sun. They thought the chiefs had the power to influence the sun. They also thought the chiefs could make important natural events, such as spring rains and the harvest, happen at the correct time. To keep their chief and rulers happy, the elites got special treatment. They had greater wealth, bigger houses, and were given special clothing and food. They did not have to work hard on the farms as commoners did.

# Conquests and Expansion

The chief was so powerful that he could command and organize a powerful army of warriors. The warriors were quick to obey his commands.

## Chiefdoms at War

Different chiefdoms sometimes fought over the most fertile areas of land. They might also attack other chiefdoms to steal their belongings or food supplies. In some cases, a chiefdom expanded by using its army to conquer new towns. They then forced the town's people to join them. To protect their homes and towns, some chiefdoms built high fences around their boundaries to keep enemies out. When a town was captured, the winners stole valuables and burned down buildings. They often put the heads of dead enemies on spikes. They also took trophies from their victims, such as **scalps**, hands, and heads.

### KNIVES FROM STONE
The Mississippian Mound Builders made sharp knives from carved stone.

# A Fighting Force

The Mississippians were the first culture in the region to produce a lot of food. With this, the populations of the chiefdoms could grow very large. This meant there were plenty of people who could fight in an army. Some people were also free to train to do other jobs, such as to be army leaders. Commoners left their fields and fought in a united chiefdom army. They worked to keep their region safe and peaceful. War also gave people a chance to improve their rank in society. Commoners could become elites by showing great skill as a warrior. That made young men want to become good warriors.

## Weapons

The main weapon was the club. These wooden clubs were about 3 feet (1 m) long, and warriors personalized their own. Some even added a row of shark's teeth down one side to make them more deadly. Warriors also used bows and arrows, and stone knives. Other knives were made from the river cane plant, which had stalks a little like bamboo.

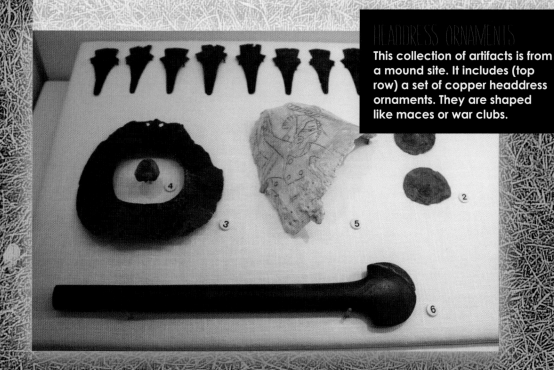

### HEADDRESS ORNAMENTS

This collection of artifacts is from a mound site. It includes (top row) a set of copper headdress ornaments. They are shaped like maces or war clubs.

# A Farmer's Life

Most commoners were farmers. Farmers were vital to the Mississippian culture. They worked hard to grow their most important and successful crop: corn.

## Farmers at Work

Farmers cleared trees to create a corn field. To make the soil ready for planting, they turned it using stone hoe blades. These blades were strapped to a handle. It is likely that they also used these small hoes for digging dirt to build the giant mounds. They often planted corn plants in raised beds of dirt. This helped to protect the plants against shallow flooding. Between the raised rows of corn, they planted beans and squash. This system did not just increase the choice of food crops. The beans used the corn stalks for support. They also returned nutrients to the soil that the corn used up. The squash plants had broad leaves, which helped keep the soil from drying out. They also reduced the number of weeds that grew.

### THE THREE SISTERS

The combination of corn, squash, and beans were very important to the ancient Mississippians. They provided most of the essential vitamins, **nutrients**, and calories needed for a healthy diet. The crops became known as the Three Sisters.

# Caring for the Corn

Crows and other animals always tried to eat the corn. So young children and people too old to do heavy farm work had the job of guarding the crops. They sat under a shelter and chased off greedy animal pests. The commoners always gave part of their harvest to the chief. That way, they secured their future. If a harvest failed, the chief could supply them with enough corn that their family could survive. By successfully farming large amounts of food, many people could stay in villages all year. That meant they did not have to move around to find food.

## ANALYZE THE ANCIENTS

These are Mississippian stone hoe blades. Can you answer these questions about what they tell us about the Mississippian Mound Builders?

1. Why do you think large groups of blades like this have been found by archaeologists?

2. What two activities that were important to the Mississippian culture were these blades used for?

# CHAPTER 3

# Settlements

There had been mound builders before the Mississippians. Some built them as lodges to live in. However, the Mississippians built theirs for special purposes. Some were for burials. Some were to build homes on for the chiefs and elite. Others were platforms to build temples on for religious ceremonies.

## Building the Mounds

Mounds were made from soil that workers dug from nearby. Groups of workers spent all the daylight hours carrying baskets of dirt. They took it to the clearing where the mound was being built. They emptied their baskets, then stamped the dirt down with their feet. That made it hard and flat. They worked for weeks before a mound-shape started to form. Most mounds were built in stages. **Generations** of workers over 100 years or more helped it reach its final height. A mound often began as a low mound with an important building on it. Sometimes, the building burned down or the important person who lived there died. Workers then brought more dirt to cover the old mound. They built up new layers, and put a new building on top.

### THRIVING CAHOKIA

This is a painting of the ancient city of Cahokia. This is how it would have looked when it was a successful and thriving center.

## Mound Styles

Mississippian towns had one or more mounds, often in the town's center. Most Mississippian mounds were roughly oval or rectangular. Mounds had a flat top that acted as a platform to build on. They could also be a stage for ceremonies. Buildings on top of the mounds were made of wooden posts. These were covered with a kind of plaster made from wet mud that dried in the sun. The roofs were **thatched**. The mounds ranged in height from 8 feet (2.4 m) to almost 100 feet (30.4 m). The base could be from 60 feet (18 m) to 770 feet (235 m) wide. People climbed to the top of the mound by a ramp or stairs up one side. Some mounds stand alone. Others are in groups of 20 or more.

# Urban Centers

A chiefdom included small villages, several larger villages, and a ceremonial town. There was a mound or mounds at the center. There were so many people in Mississippian towns that they needed to be well organized.

## Town Plans

At the center of a town, one or several mounds surrounded a plaza. The plaza served as a place for people to gather for religious ceremonies and meetings. Only chiefs built their houses and temples to their **ancestors** on mounds. They also carried out religious **rituals** on top of mounds. They buried their relatives inside mounds. This made it clear the chief was above the other people in the community. Other houses were arranged in neat rows in an area around the plaza. These homes were often lived in by several groups of relatives. Some towns had defensive structures to keep away dangerous animals or invaders. This was a wall made out of upright poles with a deep ditch outside the wall. Beyond the town were smaller villages, farmsteads, and hunting camps.

### DEFENSIVE PALISADES
Some towns built defensive wooden palisades around the buildings in the center.

**This is a reconstruction of a Mississippian Mound Builder's home from Cahokia Mounds State Historic Site in Illinois.**

# Houses and Homes

Mississippian houses were rectangular or circular. They were made from thick cane poles. The poles were set into individual holes, or along narrow **trenches**. The Mississippians made the walls by weaving canes in and out of the rows of poles. Then they coated the outside of the walls with mud that was mixed with plant fibers. Roofs were steep so rain would run off them easily. They were also covered with thatch. Roofs often had a small hole in the middle to let smoke out from winter fires. The houses had no windows, just a door. The door was covered with a blanket or woven mat to keep out cold winds. Low cane benches were built around the inner walls. These were used for seating and as beds. Woven cane mats were used for mattresses, and animal skins for bedcovers. The Mississippians stored things under the beds. They also stored things in holes in the floor, or among the rafters in the roof. They may have also painted designs on the inside and outside of their dwellings.

# Cahokia

The biggest and most important ancient Mississippian town was Cahokia. It is near what is now the city of St. Louis, Missouri. At its peak, there were as many as 20,000 people living in Cahokia. The chiefdom greatly influenced other Mississippian centers.

## Big and Busy

Cahokia consisted of about 120 mounds spread over 6 square miles (15.5 sq km). The town was laid out according to a careful plan. At the center was a huge plaza that covered nearly 40 acres (16 hectares). People met there to worship and hold ceremonies. The town was surrounded by a palisade, or pole wall, that was 2 miles (3.2 km) long. This barricade kept out enemies. It had very narrow, almost hidden openings. Only one person at a time could enter or leave through them. This meant large numbers of enemies could not get in all at once. The Mississippians could attack or capture them one by one as they came in. Most residents lived outside the palisade. Their homes were linked by courtyards and pathways. These connected homes with each other and the main town. Around the city were large farm buildings and fields. Some smaller fields and gardens were within the city, too.

### CAHOKIA MOUNDS
Around 70 mounds are preserved in Cahokia Mounds State Historic Site today.

# Monks Mound

The pyramid-shaped Monks Mound is at the center of Cahokia. It was built between AD 900 and AD 1200. Monks Mound is 100 feet (30 m) tall and covers over 6 hectares (14 acres) of land. It is one of the largest **prehistoric** earthen structures in the world. Archaeologists believe that there was a building on this mound. They believe it was 100 feet (30.5 m) long, 50 feet (15 m) wide, and 50 feet (15 m) tall. It was likely used as a meeting place for the chief, and political and religious leaders. There, they could make decisions about how to rule and **govern** Cahokia.

## ANALYZE THE ANCIENTS

This is a reconstruction of a palisade at Cahokia. Can you answer these questions about it?

1. What is the narrow opening in the palisade fence?

2. What was the main purpose of the palisade?

opening

# CHAPTER 4

# Beliefs and Rituals

The Mississippian societies shared a similar set of religious beliefs, centered on the mounds. People traveled to the town nearest them that had an important mound. They brought **offerings** to their gods, and watched ceremonies and rituals.

## The Three Worlds

The Mississippian Mound Builders believed there were three worlds. The Upper World above the sky was home to the all-powerful sun god, giver of life. It was also home to Birdman— a falcon-like figure. He ensured the triumph of day over night, life over death, and summer over winter. The Middle World was Earth, where humans lived. The ruler of the Lower World, below Earth, was named Underwater Panther. He was a wicked creature with a long tail. When he traveled to the Middle World, he turned into a great winged serpent. He then flew to the Upper World. The Mound Builders believed they had to keep the powerful forces of the Upper World and Lower World in check. They carried out rituals and ceremonies to do this. These also attracted life-renewing power from the spirit world.

**We know stone pipes made for smoking in rituals were very important. They were carved with a lot of skill. A great deal of time was taken to make them.**

## Sacred Ceremonies

The temple mound was built as a place to honor the god of the sun. Chiefs, as **descendants** of the sun, and priests performed rituals there. Commoners from the whole chiefdom watched from plazas below. There were many rituals. Some marked the passing of the seasons and others brought good harvests. For example, the chief might say prayers to ensure a good harvest. Then there would be feasts, music, dancing, and competitions. Leaders smoked sacred pipes carved with symbols of animals, such as snakes. These animals could travel between the spirit worlds. As the pipe was used, the smoke floated up into the sky as an offering to the gods. The smoke also carried people's prayers up with it.

# Death and Sacrifice

The Mississippian Mound Builders believed in an **afterlife**. They carried out ceremonies to mark a relative's passing. They buried dead relatives with valuable belongings to use in the afterlife.

## Funerals for the Chief

When a chief died, his temple was torn down or burned down. The leader's remains were then buried in the earth of the mound. Then people built up new layers of earth, increasing the height of the mound. A new building was constructed on top for the new chief. There were ceremonies and a period of **mourning**. The chief's wives and children, and the members of his close family were killed. They were then buried with him so they could go with him to the afterlife. Important people were also buried with valuables. Other people were either buried or **cremated**.

INSIDE A GRAVE

**Wealthy and important people had more items buried with them than poor people.**

This human-head pot was found at a burial site. After reading all the information on these two pages, can you answer these questions?

1. What are human head pots related to?

2. The head has tattoos or scars on the face and holes along its ears. What do these suggest?

# Human Sacrifice

The Mound Builders also carried out ritual human **sacrifices**. These were perhaps part of the ceremonies marking the death of a chief. Sacrifices gave him people to serve him in the afterlife. A mound at Cahokia contains hundreds of people. Many of them were strangled or clubbed to death on the edge of a burial pit. They then fell into it. Pots shaped like human heads are often found at the burial sites of chiefs. It is thought to relate to burial rituals or enemy sacrifice. The eyes are often closed or the person looks lifeless. They may represent dead leaders or the severed head of an enemy. Some have scars or tattoos on the face, and piercings in the ears. These are likely symbols put on people as part of important rituals in ceremonies.

# Observing the Sky

The ancient Mississippians were interested in the sun, other stars, and planets. They built monuments that were used for marking important changes in the sky. They were also used to create a calendar for their annual ceremonies and religious events.

## Celebrating the Sun

People of the Mississippian culture worshiped the sun. They held ceremonies to mark important times in the solar year. There were ceremonies for the first days of summer and winter (the solstices). There were also ceremonies for the first days of spring and fall (the equinoxes). The mounds were constructed to line up with the sun at these important times. For example, at Cahokia, the sun rises exactly over Monks Mound at the equinoxes. A chief stood on top of the temple mound for an equinox ceremony. To those gathered around below him, it looked as though he was almost bringing forth the sun. To them, it looked as though the sun shone all around him and from him.

### SOLAR ECLIPSES
The Mound Builders also held ceremonies when events such as a solar eclipse occurred.

# Solar Calendars

The Mound Builders constructed solar calendars made of huge cedar posts. They believed cedar wood to be sacred, or holy. This was possibly because the cedar tree lives for such a long time. The posts were almost 20 feet (6 m) tall. They were set into the ground and spaced evenly to form large circles. They were also painted red. The larger solar calendars, or woodhenges, were made up of 60 posts. They also had a raised platform or one post in the center. As the sun or moon passed overhead in the sky, these posts cast shadow lines. A priest standing in the middle could tell the time of year, based on where the sun rose and set. These posts were likely used as a kind of calendar. The posts marked the solstices, equinoxes, and festivals important to the Mound Builders.

**WOODHENGES**

**Solar calendars were called "woodhenges" in reference to Stonehenge. It is a huge stone solar calendar found in England.**

# CHAPTER 5

# Trade and Treasures

The Mississippian Mound Builders traded up and down the Mississippi River. They traded from coast to coast and from north to south. Archaeologists have found materials at Cahokia that suggest the city traded with peoples from far away. These items were from the Gulf of Mexico, the Appalachians, the Great Lakes, and the Rocky Mountains.

## On the Move

Mississippian Mound Builders used dugout canoes made from pine or cypress tree trunks. They were used to travel up and down the river. These canoes could carry a large amount of goods for trade. The largest were big enough to hold 60 to 70 people, sitting in three rows. They were long and narrow, so they could capsize, or tip over, easily. But they could move quite quickly if the oarsmen were strong. People also moved them along using poles. They pushed the poles against the river bottom if the water was very calm or shallow. When they had to leave these heavy boats at the shore, they turned the boats over. The layer of bark on the outside fooled would-be thieves into thinking they were just fallen trees.

### TRAVELING BY WATER

The Mound Builders sometimes used rafts for short-distance travel. But they mainly used dugout canoes like this one to travel for trade.

# Trading for Treasures

Elite Mississippians wanted valuable treasures for ornaments to show off their wealth. They gave them as gifts to other chiefdoms to form bonds. There were also given to keep peace with them. There was a constant demand for more luxury items. These were either traded with other groups, or made from materials brought from far away. In the marketplace in Cahokia, people exchanged many things. White-tailed deer hides or salt from nearby mines were traded for sea shells from the Gulf of Mexico. Chert, a flintlike rock, came from Oklahoma. Through trade, the different chiefdoms also exchanged ideas. Objects from Mississippian times have been found in mounds of chiefdoms over a wide area. They all share the same designs and symbols.

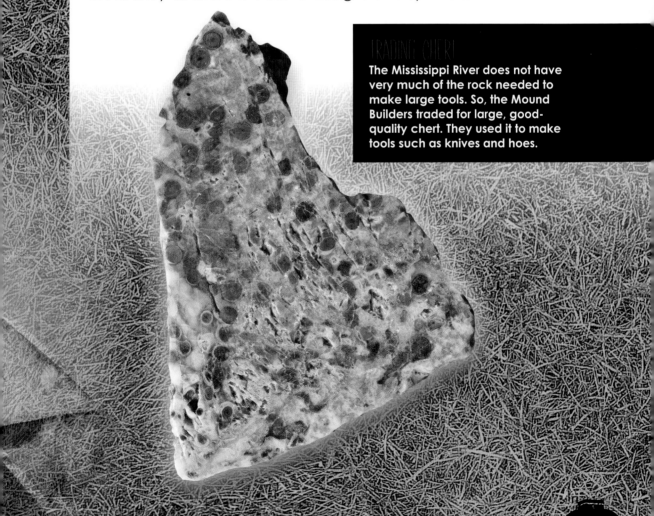

## TRADING CHERT

The Mississippi River does not have very much of the rock needed to make large tools. So, the Mound Builders traded for large, good-quality chert. They used it to make tools such as knives and hoes.

# Symbols and Shells

Many of the items made by the Mound Builders had symbols linked to their beliefs. Some animals move between land and water or land and sky. They were seen as messengers between people on Earth, and the Upper World and Lower World.

## Copper Crafts

Mississippian people most likely traded for raw copper like their Woodland ancestors had. It came from the Great Lakes area. Copper workshops were in centers such as Cahokia. Craftspeople pounded nuggets of raw copper into flat sheets. Then they cut and hammered it into bracelets, rings, or ear spools (ornaments worn in the earlobe). They also heated it and shaped it into beads. On some items, they embossed, or pressed, important symbols such as the sun or animals. These included falcons and other birds of prey. These animals could move between the Upper World of the sky and the Middle World of Earth.

### COPPER TREASURES

**An artist from the Mississippi Mound Builders made this bird image. It was made from a flattened sheet of copper.**

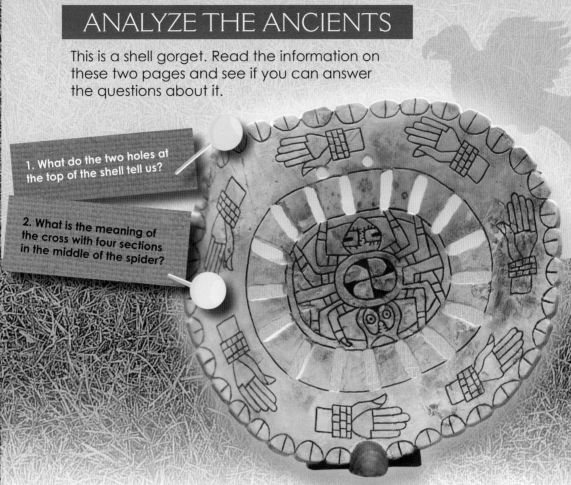

This is a shell gorget. Read the information on these two pages and see if you can answer the questions about it.

1. What do the two holes at the top of the shell tell us?

2. What is the meaning of the cross with four sections in the middle of the spider?

# Secrets in the Shells

Sea shells, such as whelks or conchs, were carved and polished into pendants, called gorgets. These hung from a string and were worn on the chest. These valuable gorgets were worn by chiefs and the elite. They were often shaped like the sun and decorated with important symbols, such as spiders. The spider was believed to have carried the first fire to humans. It also represents weaving, fertility, balance, and harmony. There was also often a cross with four sections in the middle. This is a symbol of fire, the sun, the center of the earth. It could also represent the four directions: north, south, east, and west. The body of the spider also forms a kind of cross, with four groups of two legs.

# A New Kind of Pottery

The Mississippians produced ceramics and pottery with creative and artistic designs. They were made to last. Potters were mainly women. The pottery they made was more advanced than that made by their ancestors. They used a new technique that made it very special.

## Mixed with Shells

The Mound Builder potters made ceramics from clay and mussel shells. These materials had been burned and crushed into tiny pieces. This new mixture produced a kind of ceramic that was stronger. So, it could be used to make thinner pots that spread heat more evenly when used for cooking. The shell-mixed clay was rolled into long, thin sausages. They were then coiled one on top of the other to make pots. The completed pot was then smoothed before being stood by a wood fire to dry and harden. It was then fired on the coals as the fire died down.

**POTS THAT LAST**

**Mound Builders made strong pots designed to last. This bowl is in the shape of a human. It was found in a burial mound in Tennessee.**

# Using the Ceramics

Before this new kind of clay was created, most pots were chunky. They were made mainly for cooking or storing food. The new ceramics could be made in a variety of shapes and designs. The could be used in ceremonies or as a show of wealth for the elite.

Ceramics made for ceremonies had designs stamped or pressed into the sides. This was done before they were fired. Sometimes, the pots were painted red. Some bowls or jars were made in human or animal forms. There are animal pots in the form of bears, possums, beavers, ducks, owls, fish, and dogs. Special pottery bottles were made for a drink made from roasted holly leaves. People drank it in large amounts very quickly to make themselves vomit. They believed this made them clean and pure. They were then ready to perform or take part in special ceremonies.

# CHAPTER 6

# Everyday Life

What everyday life was like for the Mound Builders depended on whether they were a girl or a boy, a man or a woman. Archaeologists can tell a lot about these differences by what they found buried in women's and men's graves. For example, they found cooking pots for women, and axes and fishhooks for men.

## Farming, Cooking, and Crafting

Women and girls spent much of their time near the home. After preparing and eating breakfast, they tended the crops in the fields. They also gathered firewood or berries in the forest. They looked after the house, made pottery, and wove mats and fabrics. They often worked in the small courtyards and gardens outside a group of homes. Every day, women and girls pounded corn, nuts, beans, and seeds into meal and flour. To do this, they put them into a big **mortar** made from a hollow tree trunk. They used a pounder made from a smoothed, rounded ash log to pound and crush them.

### POT MAKERS

As well as taking care of the home, it was women's job to make the pots. Mound Builders used pots for storing, cooking, and serving food.

# Hunting and Fishing

Boys and men prepared fields and harvested crops. They also gave their time as **tribute** to the chief by clearing trees or building mounds. They also spent hours hunting. From a young age, boys learned to track, stalk, and kill wild animals. They usually used a bow and arrows. They sometimes used **blowguns** and darts. They grew skilled at creeping up on animals quietly. They had to get close enough to ensure they would hit their target. Some even wore deer masks to help them get close to their prey. Hunters often went out in small groups. They carried a bag of charms for good luck, and some dried corn and seeds to snack on. They sometimes stayed in hunting camps. There, they skinned and cut up animals, then took the meat home. Before hunting, they often held a ceremony to pray for a good hunt. After they killed an animal, they said prayers to ask for forgiveness for taking a life. Men taught boys how to fish using spears and nets. They also showed them how to use basket cages.

## HUNTING TOOLS

**Experts think this bird stone was used to help Mississippian hunters. They used it to hurl a short spear from a throwing stick with greater force.**

# Mississippian Style

We can learn what Mississippian Mound Builders looked like and what they wore. We can study the objects they left behind. These include carved stone figures and engravings on sea shells. They show people wearing different types of clothing, hairstyles, and ornaments.

## Clothing

Mississippian clothing was very simple. Men wore only a breechcloth. This was a rectangular piece of deerskin, cloth, or animal fur. It was worn between the legs and folded over a belt. The flaps fell in front and behind. In cold weather, they added long deerskin leggings and tunics. Women wore skirts of deerskin, or cloth woven from tree bark. In cold weather, they also wore a wrap. They used dyes to paint or color their clothes, and they decorated them, too. Some elites wore ornate and colorful shawls or cloaks. These were sometimes decorated with shells or feathers. Women usually wore their hair long. They sometimes braided it or tied it back with hair ornaments. Sometimes, men completely shaved the hair from one side of their head. They kept it long on the other side.

### ELITE MAN

This diorama shows an elite man from Cahokia. He is wearing a cloth skirt and sash, an engraved shell gorget, and ear spools. He also has a falcon eye design painted on his face.

# Body Decorations

It is believed that many women decorated themselves. They blackened their teeth with ashes from cold fires. They also rubbed red powder onto their faces, shoulders, and stomachs. This powder was made by grinding a red rock. Men often had more body decorations than women, especially for religious ceremonies. For ceremonies, they might cover themselves with red, white, or black markings, and tie feathers in their hair. Men and women wore ornaments called ear spools. These required quite large piercings in their earlobes. They also wore necklaces made of shells or seeds. The elites and the best warriors wore red-and-black tattoos on their faces and other parts of their bodies. These were often in symbolic designs. The chief might also wear fancy feather headdresses during religious festivals.

**MISSISSIPPIAN BEADS**

**Necklaces of shells were commonly worn. Sometimes, strings of beads were also worn around the wrists and ankles.**

37

# Feasts and Food

The Mississippian Mound Builders ate corn, squash, and beans every day, but they also ate a mix of other foods. Some they farmed. Others they gathered or caught in the wild.

## Wild Foods

The Mississippian men hunted a variety of animals. These included rabbits, muskrats, beavers, deer, and turkeys. Deer meat was a favorite food. They also dried the meat on racks over smoky fires. In the fall, they hunted for bears. The bears had put on lots of fat to survive the cold winter ahead. The Mississippians used bear fat for cooking. In the summer, they collected fruits such as wild grapes, persimmons, and pawpaws. In the fall, they gathered nuts such as chestnuts, pecans, and hickory nuts. Hickory nuts were boiled to get oil that they used in cooking. They caught large numbers of ducks from the water using nets. They also caught turtles and catfish. They caught other large fish in the lakes that formed on the slow bends of the river and its **tributaries**. They often fished with spears or nets. They also caught fish in basket cages made from the hard but flexible stems of the river cane plant. It was a little like bamboo.

### DRYING FISH

The Mississippians likely hung some of the fish that they caught out in the sun to dry. This was so that they could store it and eat it later.

**The Mississippian Mound Builders collected wild fruits such as pawpaws to eat. Their name for the pawpaw was "umbi."**

# Cooking and Eating

Women tended to do the cooking. Like the men, they spent most of their day outside, and cooking was done outside, too. Fresh corn was mixed with beans, squash, and other vegetables such as wild onions and leeks. These were made into healthy stews. These stews bubbled away over fires all day. People dipped big ladles into it when they were hungry. Corn flour and meal was mixed with bear fat. It was then cooked on a hot rock by the fire to make cakes. They also roasted meats such as bear, deer, and turkey over a fire.

# A Day at the Games

Most days were the same for the Mound Builders. So they must have looked forward to the religious festivals that broke up their routine. They also enjoyed watching chunkey. This was a ritual and highly competitive game.

## The Culture of Chunkey

Chunkey was a game likely invented by people in Cahokia. It was probably taught to other Mississippians whom they fought and traded with. The Mississippians believed chunkey was created by the spirit beings. In the culture's oldest stories, it was played by the chiefs and the elite. Chunkey was played in huge fields in the towns. People came from villages and farms all over the chiefdom to watch the games. The games could go on for hours. Only men could play. Players from other towns came to challenge the local players. Lots of people gambled and bet their belongings on who would be the winner.

## Playing the Game

The game was played with a stone disk about the size of a modern hockey puck. The disk was rolled across a playing field. Competing players had to throw poles at the point where they guessed the disk would stop. The pole closest to its final position, without actually hitting it, was the winner. The game taught Mississippian hunters and warriors to figure out the speed and distance of a moving object. They had to do this quickly so they could aim at moving animals or enemies accurately. The game was so important that only chunkey players were featured in Mississippian carvings. No other athletes playing other sports were shown.

# ANALYZE THE ANCIENTS

This is an ancient Mississippian stone carving showing a chunkey player about to release the stone disk. It was carved in Cahokia, but found near Ocumulgee, Oklahoma. Can you answer these questions about it?

1. What does the fact it was made in one place and found in another tell us?

2. What does the fact that only chunkey players were shown in Mississippian carvings tell us?

# Disease and Decline

The Mississippian Mound Builders had created a highly successful culture. But they began to decline from about 1400 BC to 1450 BC. By the time European explorers arrived, the Mississippian Mound Builder culture was already over. Archaeologists believe that this great society collapsed for a variety of reasons.

## In Trouble

Experts believe that the Mississippians hunted all the animals in the area and used up all of the trees. Without forests, the animals they once hunted would be gone and they would be left with little food. After many years of planting similar crops in their fields, the soil may have been robbed of its nutrients. It would no longer be fertile enough. Their troubles may also have been caused by periods of drought, floods, and winter frosts. Those would have ruined their harvests and affected the plants and animals in the region. Archaeologists have found the remains of very thin bodies. This suggests that people were starving or possibly suffered from diseases. Diseases would have spread quickly through people living close together in towns.

ARRIVAL OF HERNANDO DE SOTO

This engraving shows Spanish explorer Hernando de Soto arriving at the Mississippi River in 1541. Early European explorers brought diseases. The diseases devestated populations of Native Americans across the Southeast.

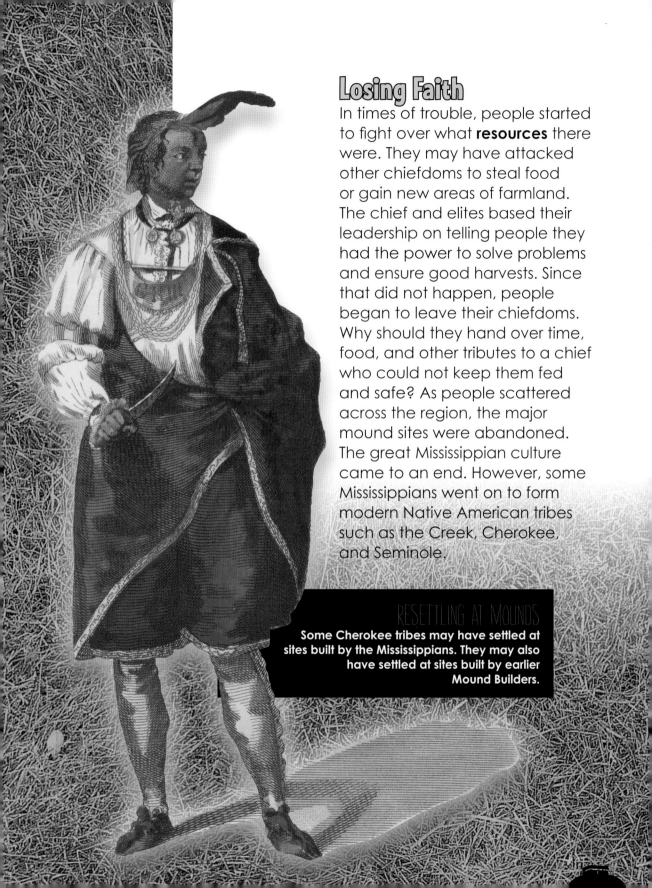

# Losing Faith

In times of trouble, people started to fight over what **resources** there were. They may have attacked other chiefdoms to steal food or gain new areas of farmland. The chief and elites based their leadership on telling people they had the power to solve problems and ensure good harvests. Since that did not happen, people began to leave their chiefdoms. Why should they hand over time, food, and other tributes to a chief who could not keep them fed and safe? As people scattered across the region, the major mound sites were abandoned. The great Mississippian culture came to an end. However, some Mississippians went on to form modern Native American tribes such as the Creek, Cherokee, and Seminole.

## RESETTLING AT MOUNDS

Some Cherokee tribes may have settled at sites built by the Mississippians. They may also have settled at sites built by earlier Mound Builders.

# Answers

Did you manage to analyze the ancients? Check your answers against the correct answers on these pages.

## PAGE 9

1. The fact that the statue was found in a temple tells us that it was used in Mississippian religious ceremonies.
2. The corn suggests the statue was part of a corn ceremony. It also tells us that corn was important to the Mississippian Mound Builders' lives.

## PAGE 15

1. Large numbers of stone hoe blades have been found because farming was such an important activity for the Mississippians. Most commoners were farmers.
2. Stone hoes were used for farming but also for digging dirt to build the giant mounds. The hoe blades are small, so it must have taken years to build the mounds. It must also have been hard, slow work.

## PAGE 21

1. The narrow opening in the palisade fence is an entrance.
2. The main purpose of the palisade was defense. The entrance was very narrow so that only one person could enter or leave at one time. This ensured that large numbers of enemies could not get in all at once. The residents could attack or capture the enemies one by one as they came in.

## PAGE 25

1. Pots shaped like human heads are often found at the burial sites of chiefs. They are thought to relate to burial rituals or enemy sacrifice.
2. The scar or tattoo lines and piercings are likely to be symbols put on people as part of important rituals in ceremonies.

# Answers

PAGE 31

1. The two holes in the gorget tell us it hung from a string, so it could be worn on the chest.
2. The cross in the middle is a symbol of fire, the sun, the center of Earth, or the four directions north, south, east, and west.

PAGE 41

1. It tells us that chunkey was likely invented by people in Cahokia. It was probably taught to other Mississippians who they fought and traded with.
2. There are no images of athletes playing other sports shown in Mississippian carvings. This tells us that chunkey must have been very important to the Mound Builders.

# Glossary

**afterlife** life after death

**ancestors** relatives from long ago

**artifacts** objects from the past that tell us about people's lives in history

**blowguns** tubes through which darts are forced by blowing air in fast

**chiefdom** an area ruled by a chief

**civilization** a settled and stable community in which people live together peacefully and use systems such as writing to communicate

**cremated** disposed of a dead body by burning it to ashes, usually after a funeral ceremony

**culture** the beliefs, customs, and arts of a particular group or country of people

**descendants** children, grandchildren, and so on, who are related to a particular person

**elite** the highest class of people in certain societies

**fertile** describes soil that is full of nutrients so plants grow well in it

**generations** all the people born and living at about the same time

**govern** to control, lead, or be in charge of an area or a people

**mortar** a hard, bowl-shaped object in which substances are pounded

**mourning** expressing sorrow for someone's death

**nutrients** substances plants and animals need to be healthy and to grow well

**offerings** things that people give as part of a religious ceremony or ritual

**prehistoric** a time before written historical records began

**ranks** positions of importance in an army, society, or other group

**resources** things that can be used or made into new things, such as water and rock

**rituals** religious ceremonies

**sacrifices** people or animals killed to honor a god or gods

**scalps** the part of the human head that has the hair attached

**society** a large group of people living together in an organized way

**staple** food that is very important in a culture's diet

**symbols** images that represent something else

**temples** buildings where people go to worship their god or gods

**thatched** covered a roof with straw, reeds, or similar plants

**trenches** long, narrow ditches

**tributaries** rivers or streams flowing into a larger river or lake

**tribute** a gift of food or other items paid by people to their ruler

# For More Information

## Books

Gear, W. Michael and Kathleen O'Neil Gear. *People of the Weeping Eye: Book One of the Moundville Duology*. New York, NY: Tor books, 2008.

Gibson, Karen Bush. *Native American History for Kids: With 21 Activities*. Chicago, IL: Chicago Review Press, 2010.

Griggs, Howard. *The Native American Mound Builders*. Rosen Classroom, 2013.

Iseminger, William. *Cahokia Mounds: America's First City*. Charleston, SC: The History Press, 2010.

## Websites

Discover more about the Mound Builders at:
**www.nps.gov/nr/travel/mounds/builders.htm**

Learn more about Cahokia at:
**cahokiamounds.org**

Read about the Mississippian culture at:
**nativeamericans.mrdonn.org/southeast/mississippians.html**

Find out more about the Mississippian Mound Builders at:
**www.warpaths2peacepipes.com/native-american-houses/mound-builders.html**

# Index